THIS BOOK BELONGS TO:

....

....

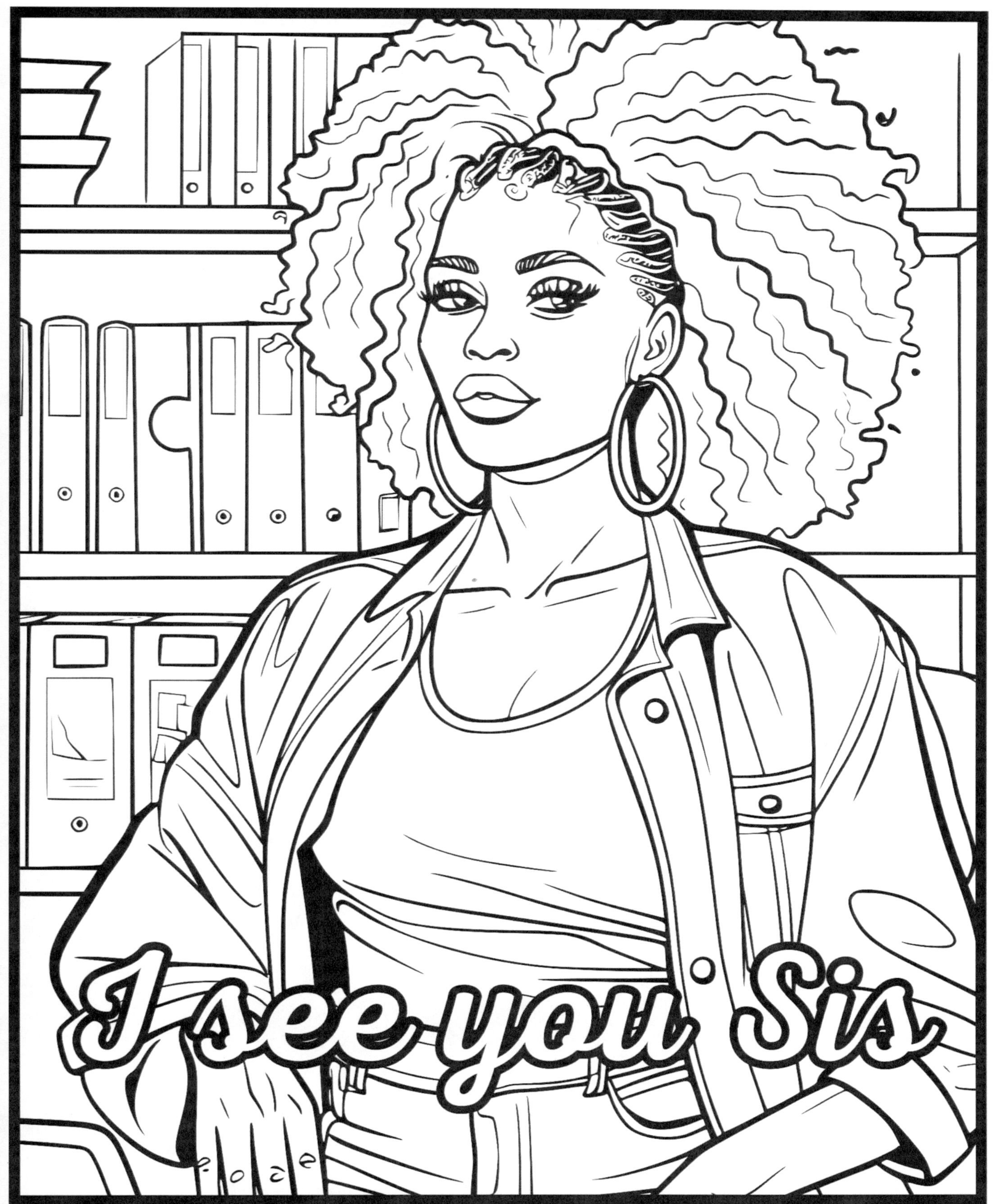

I see you Sis

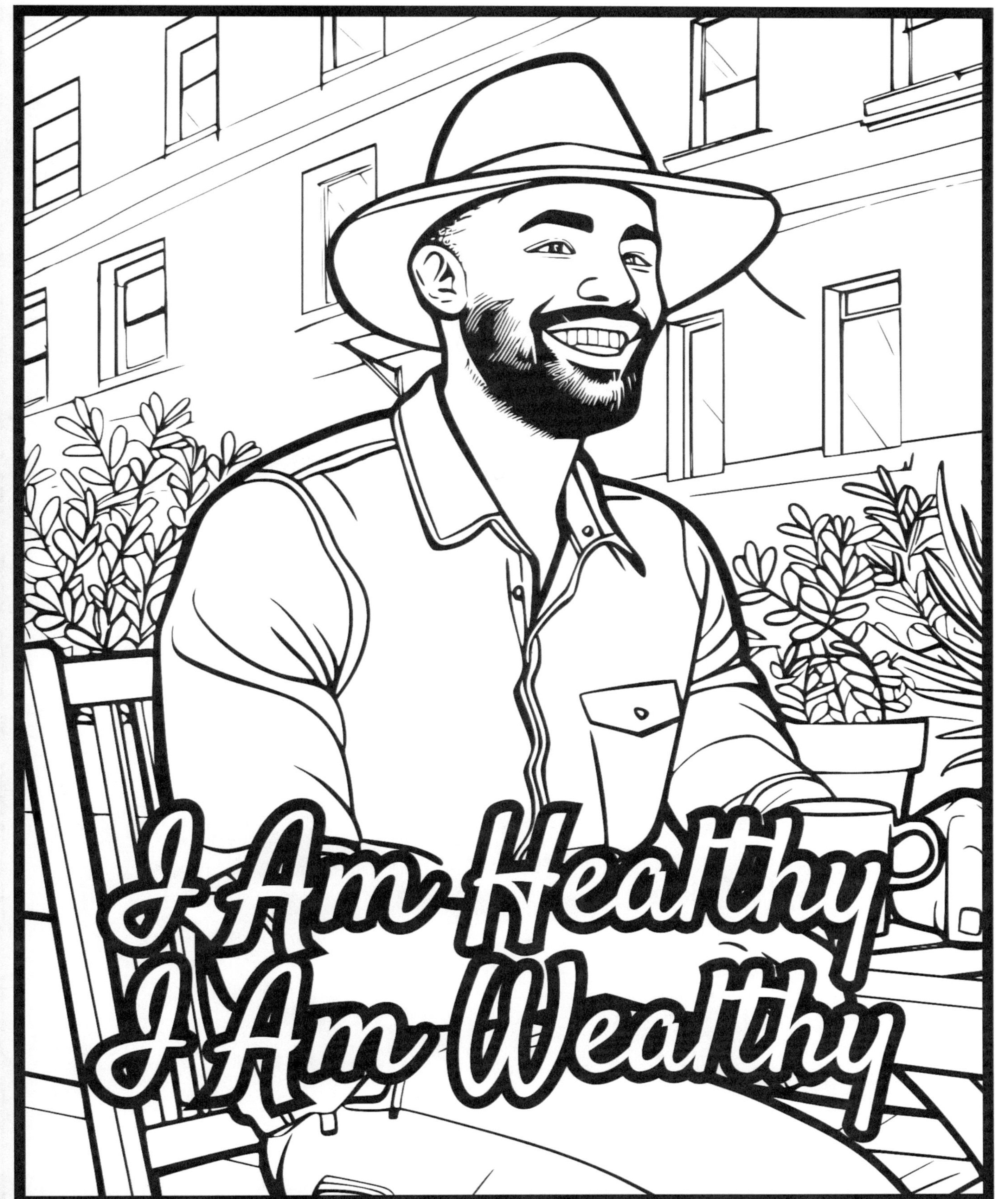

I Am Healthy
I Am Wealthy

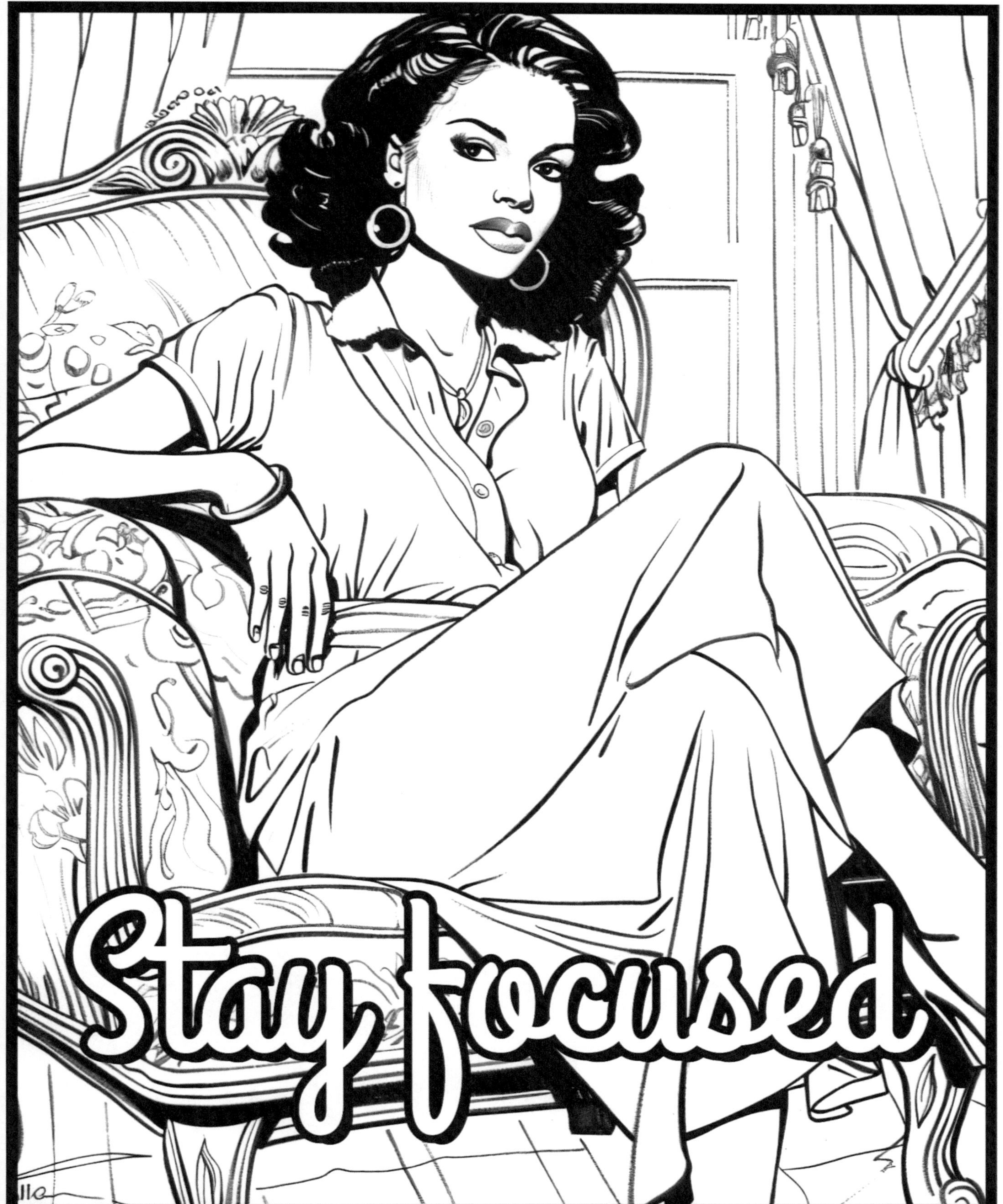

Stay focused

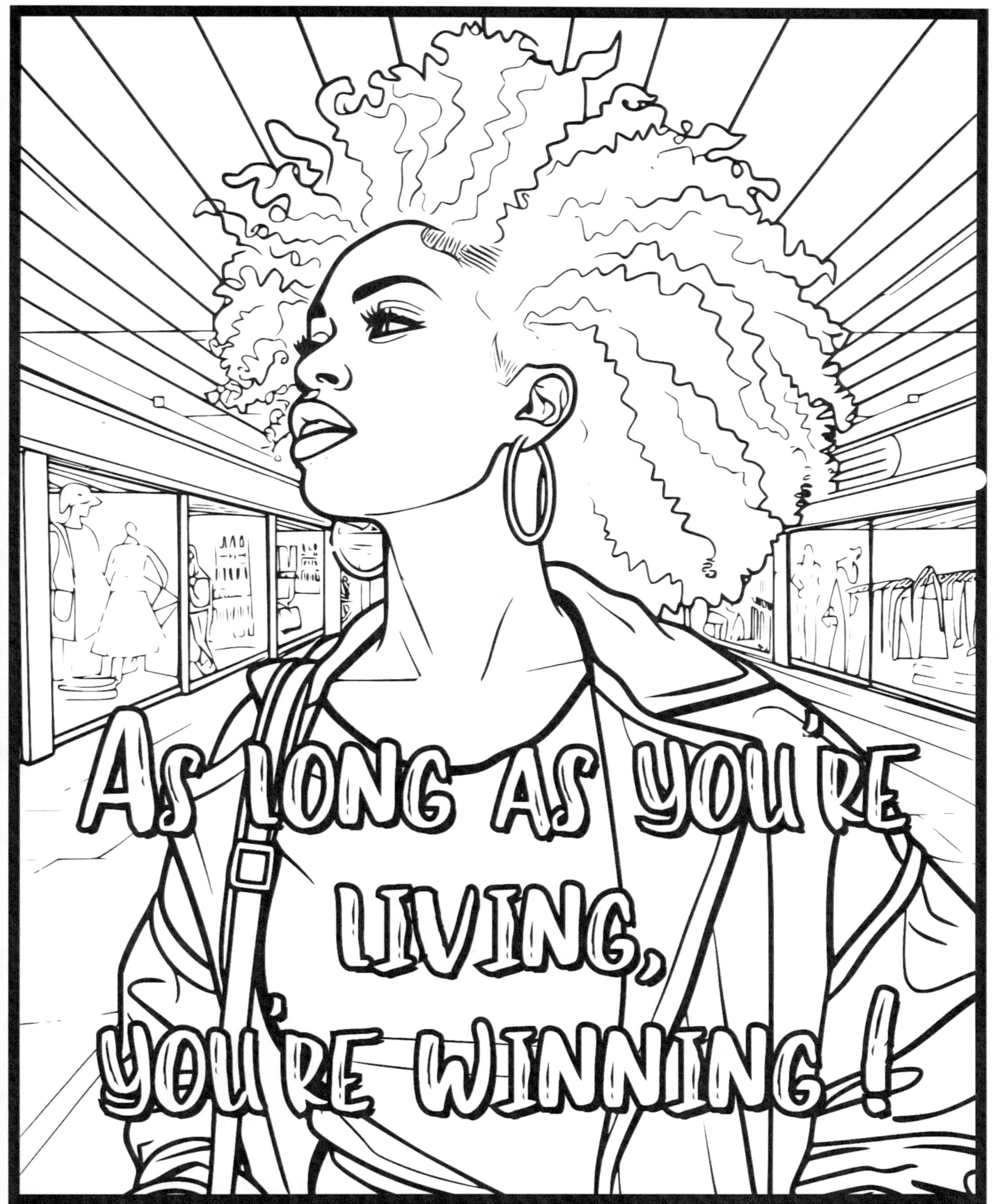

As long as you're living,
you're winning!

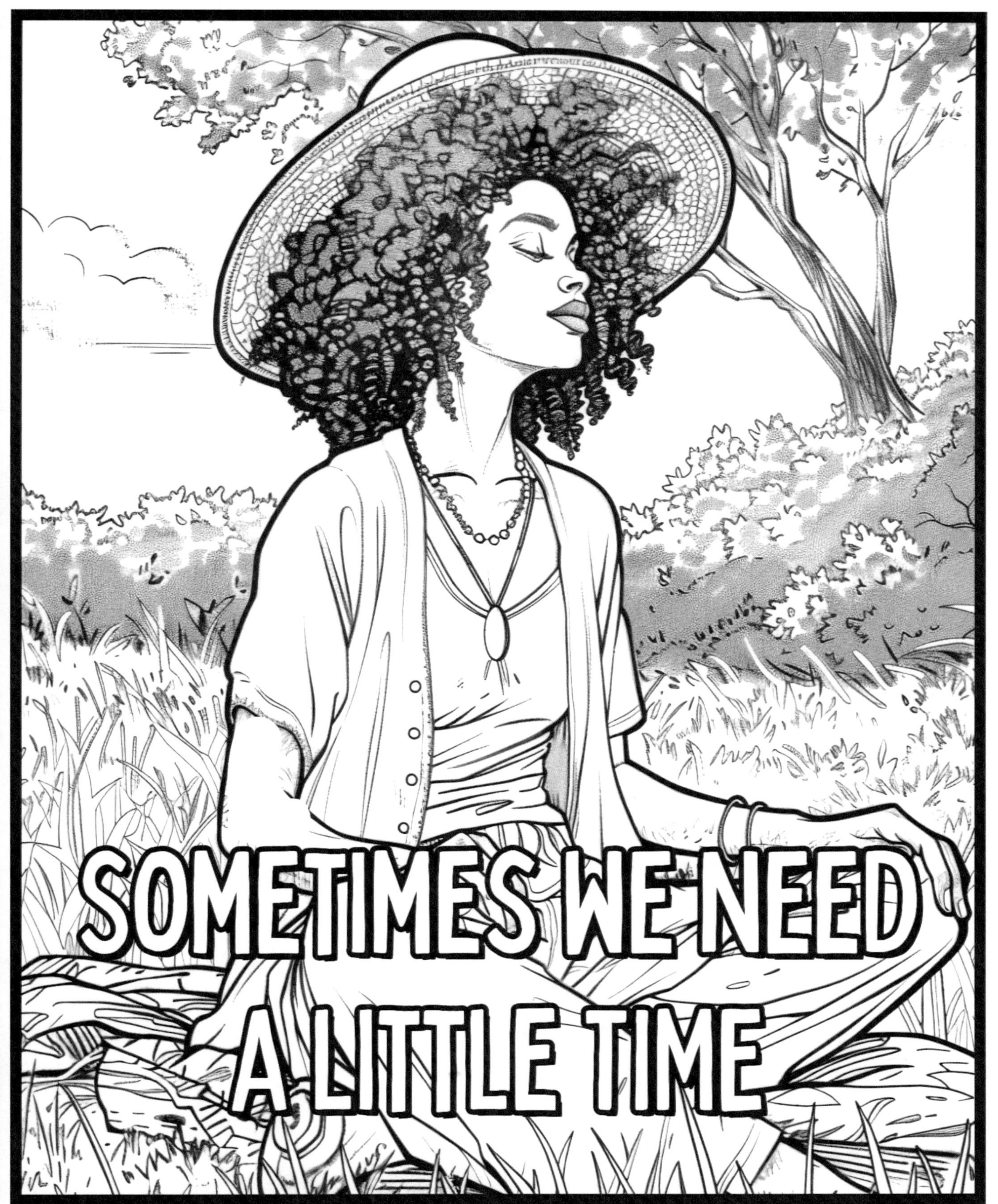

SOMETIMES WE NEED
A LITTLE TIME

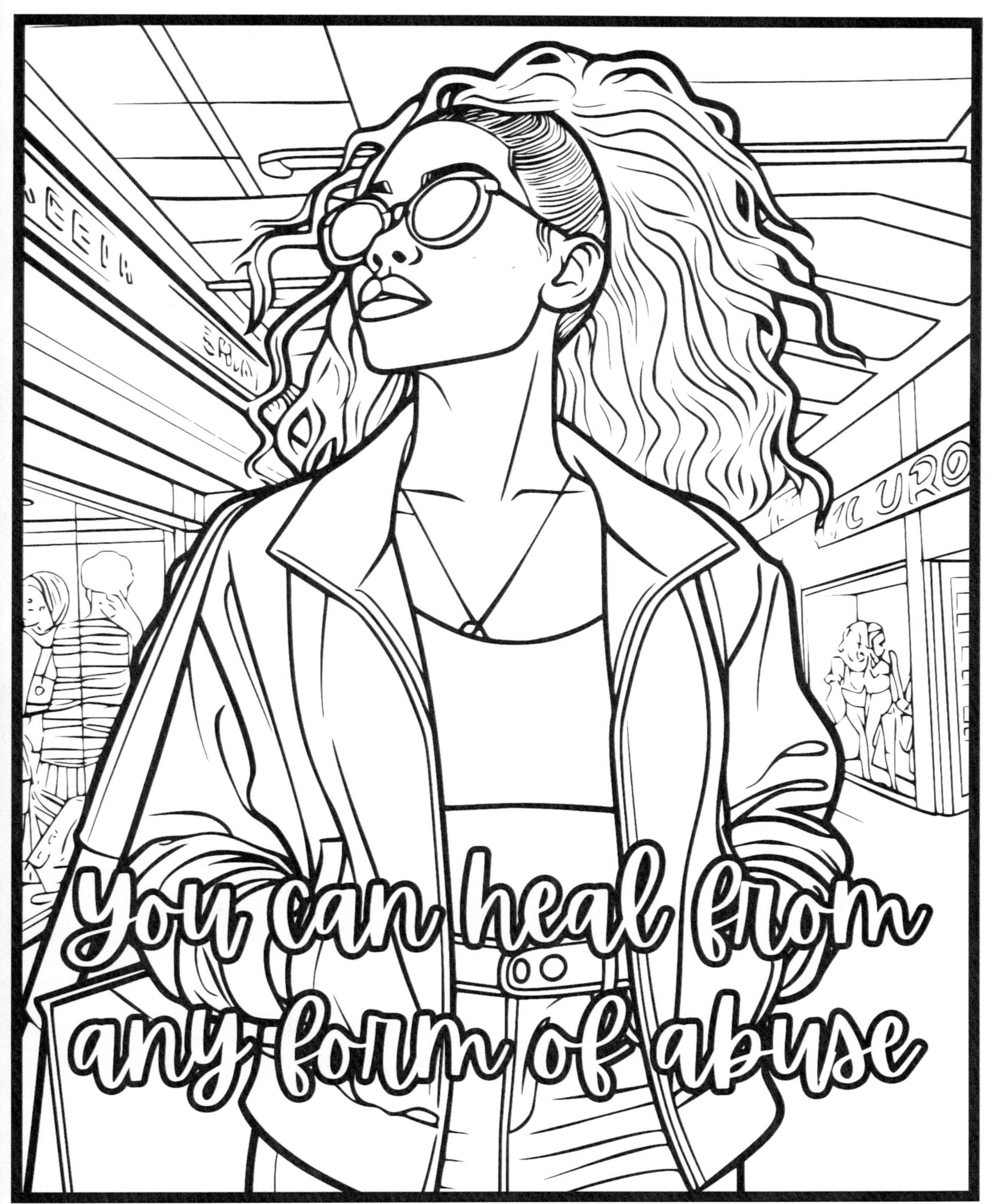
You can heal from
any form of abuse

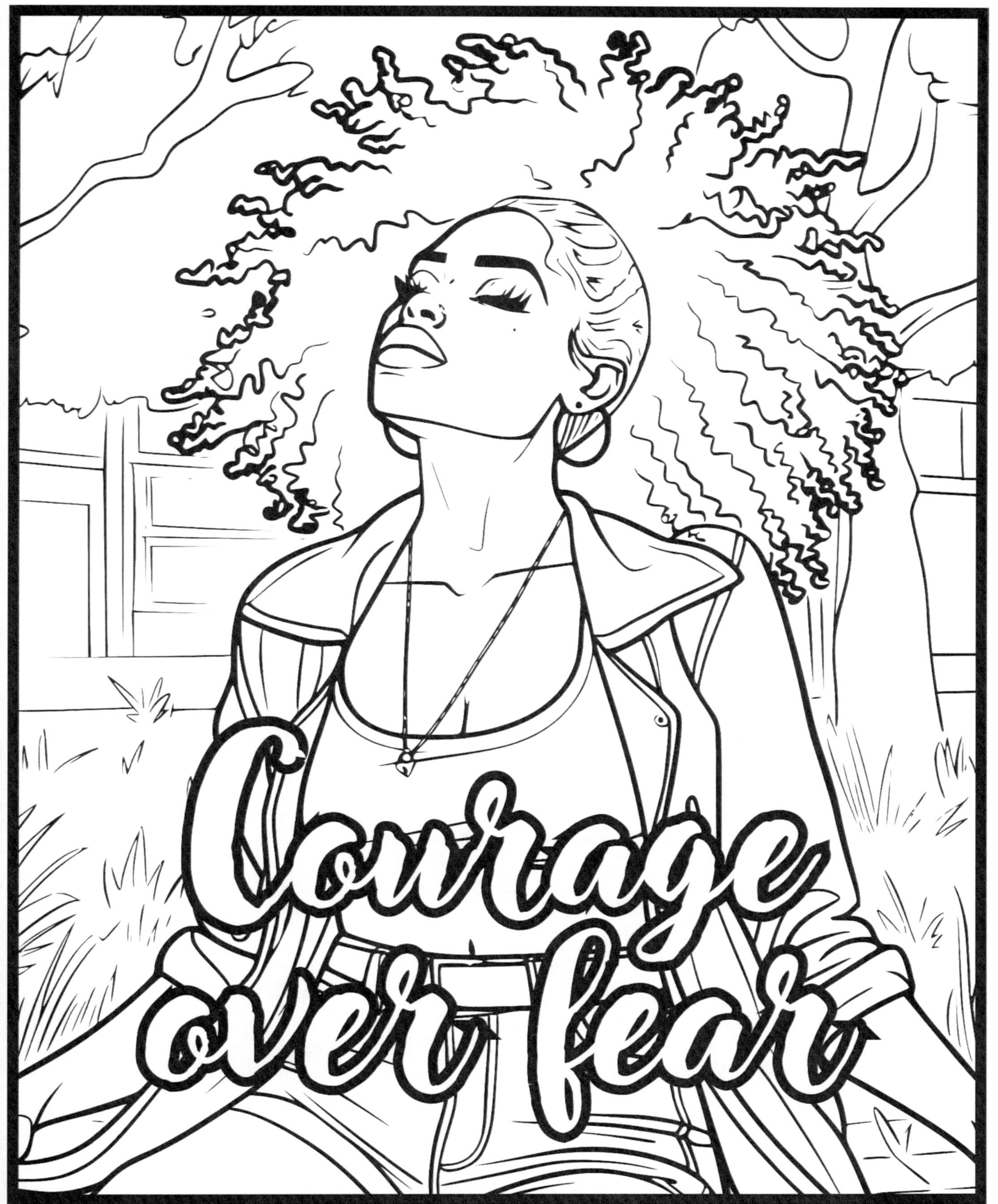

Courage
over fear

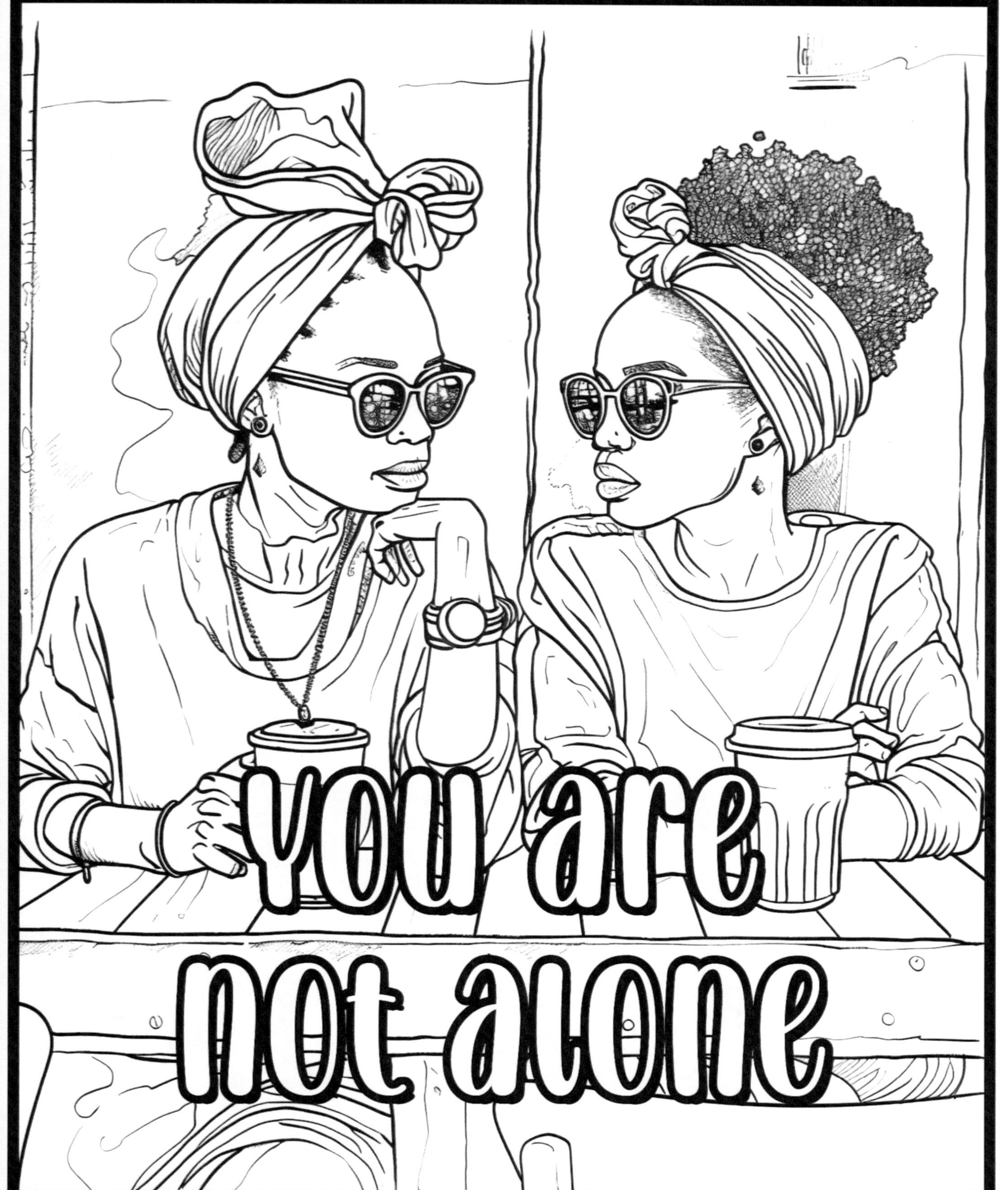

you are
not alone

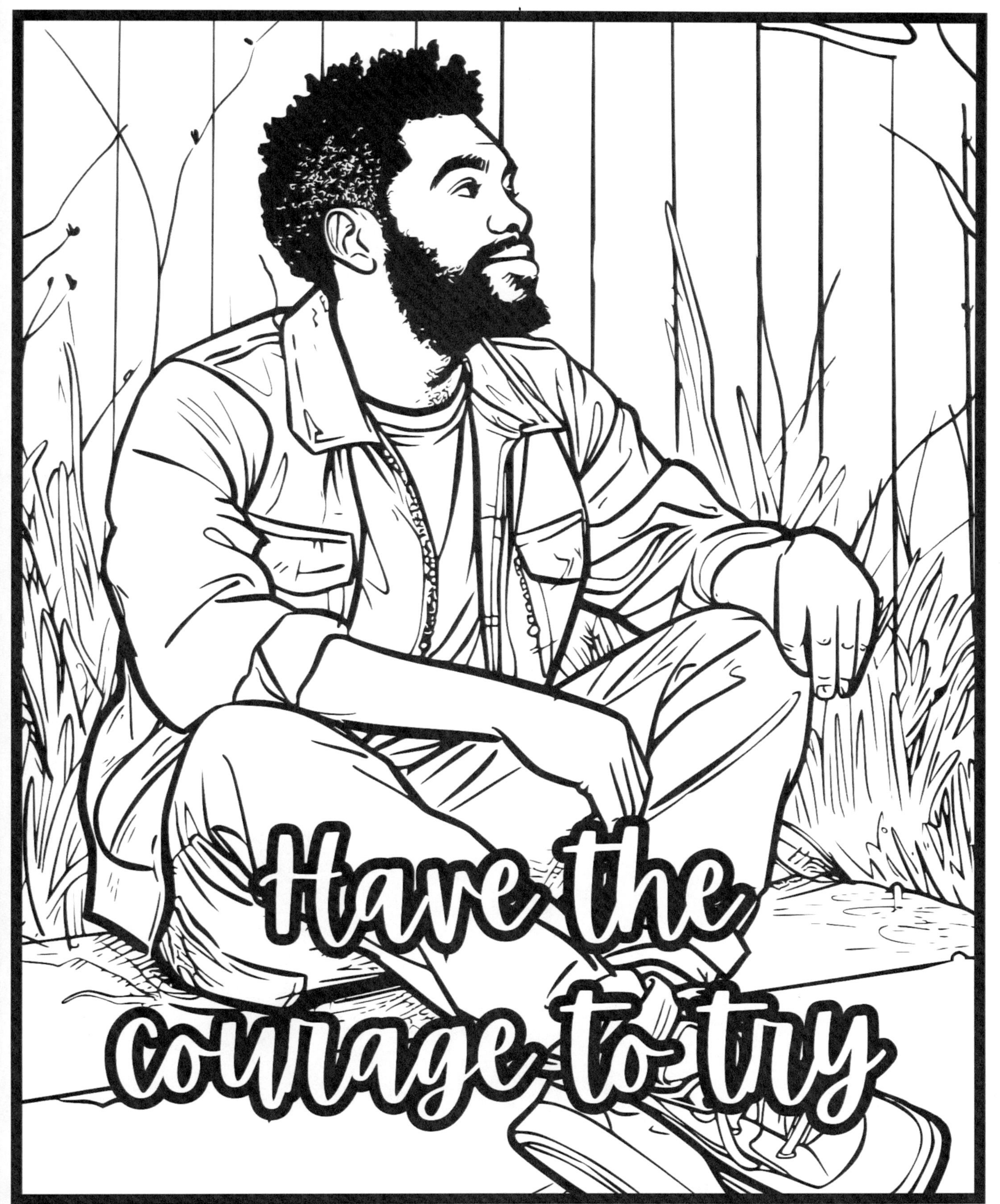
Have the
courage to try

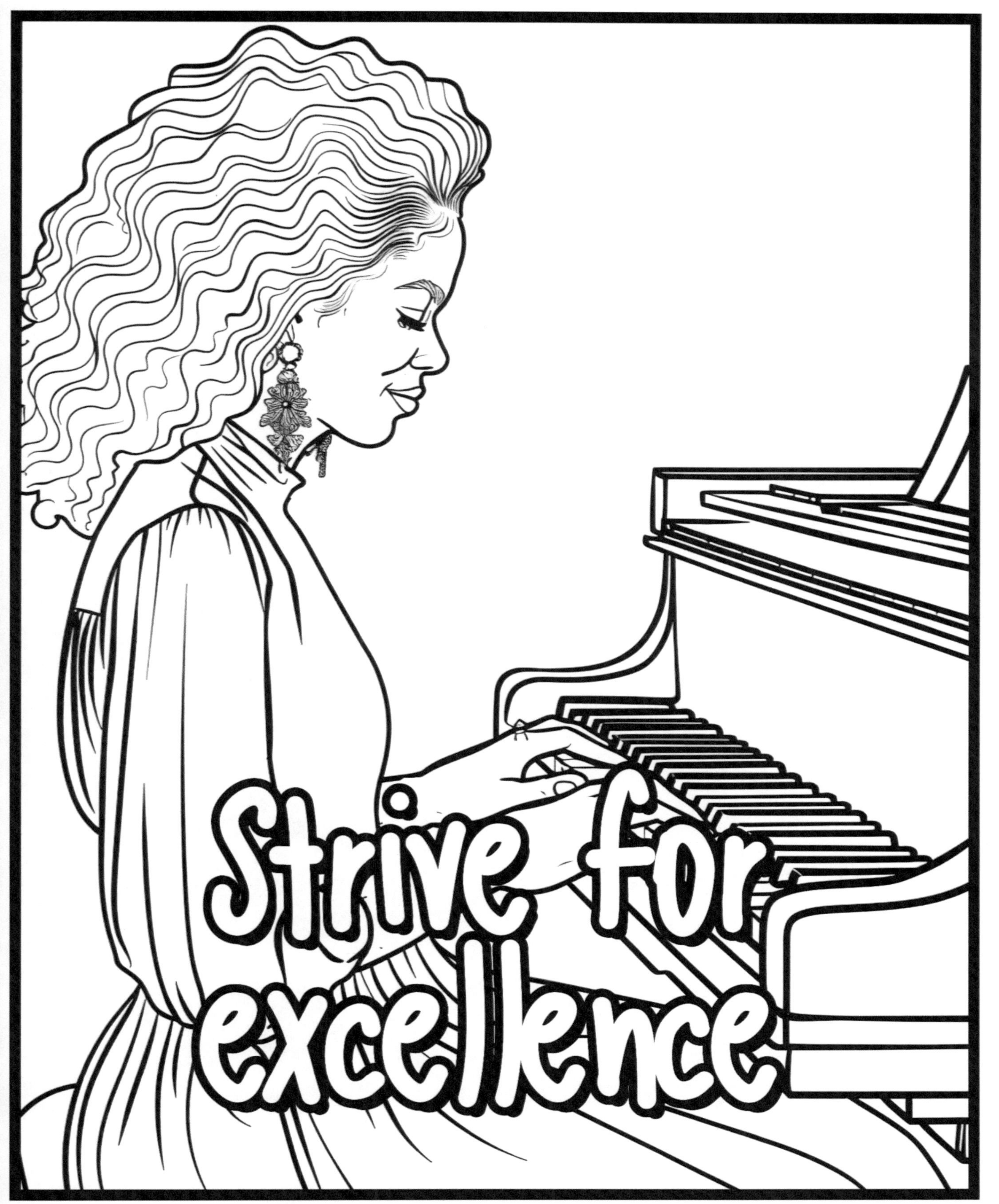

Strive for
excellence

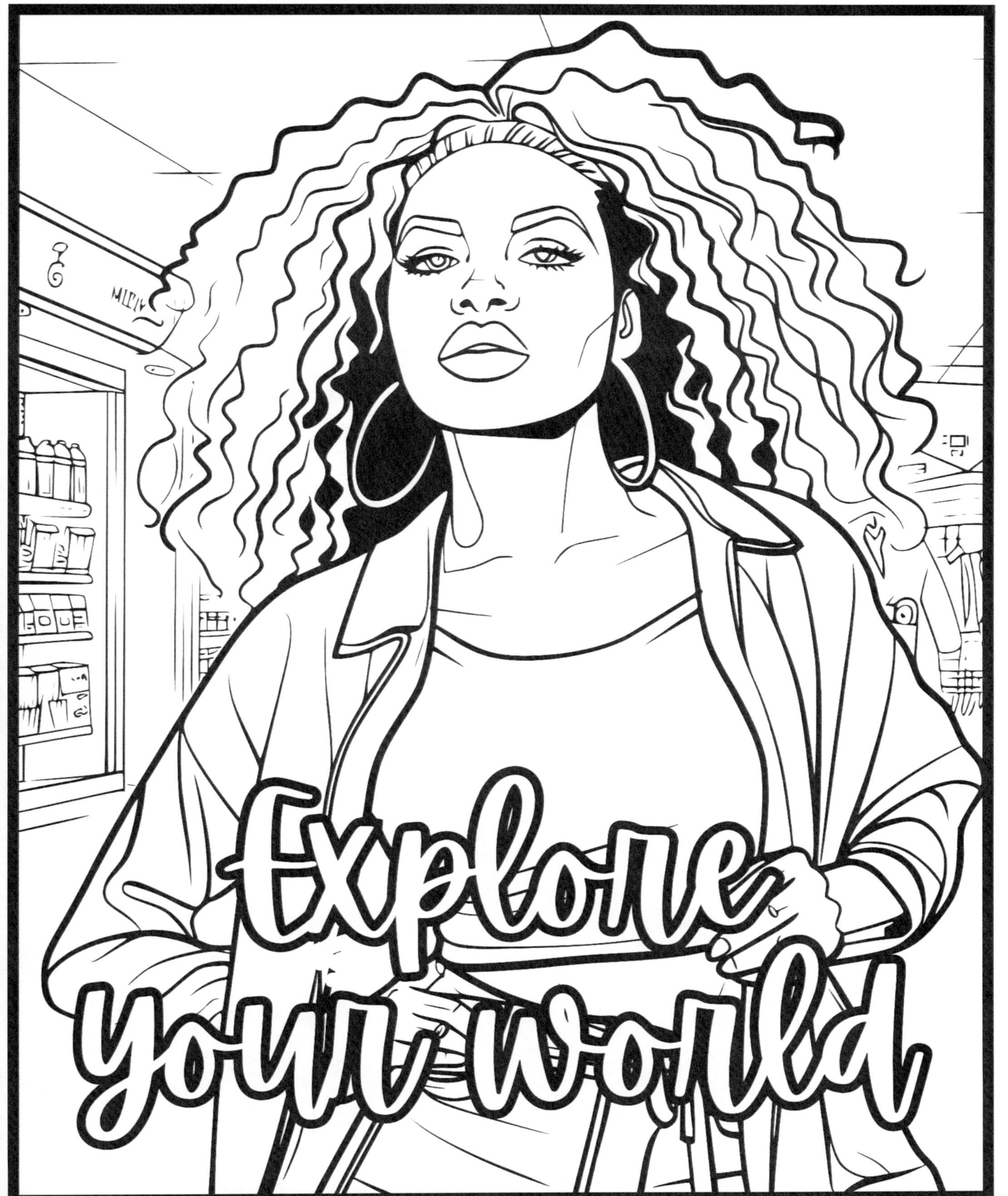

Explore
your world

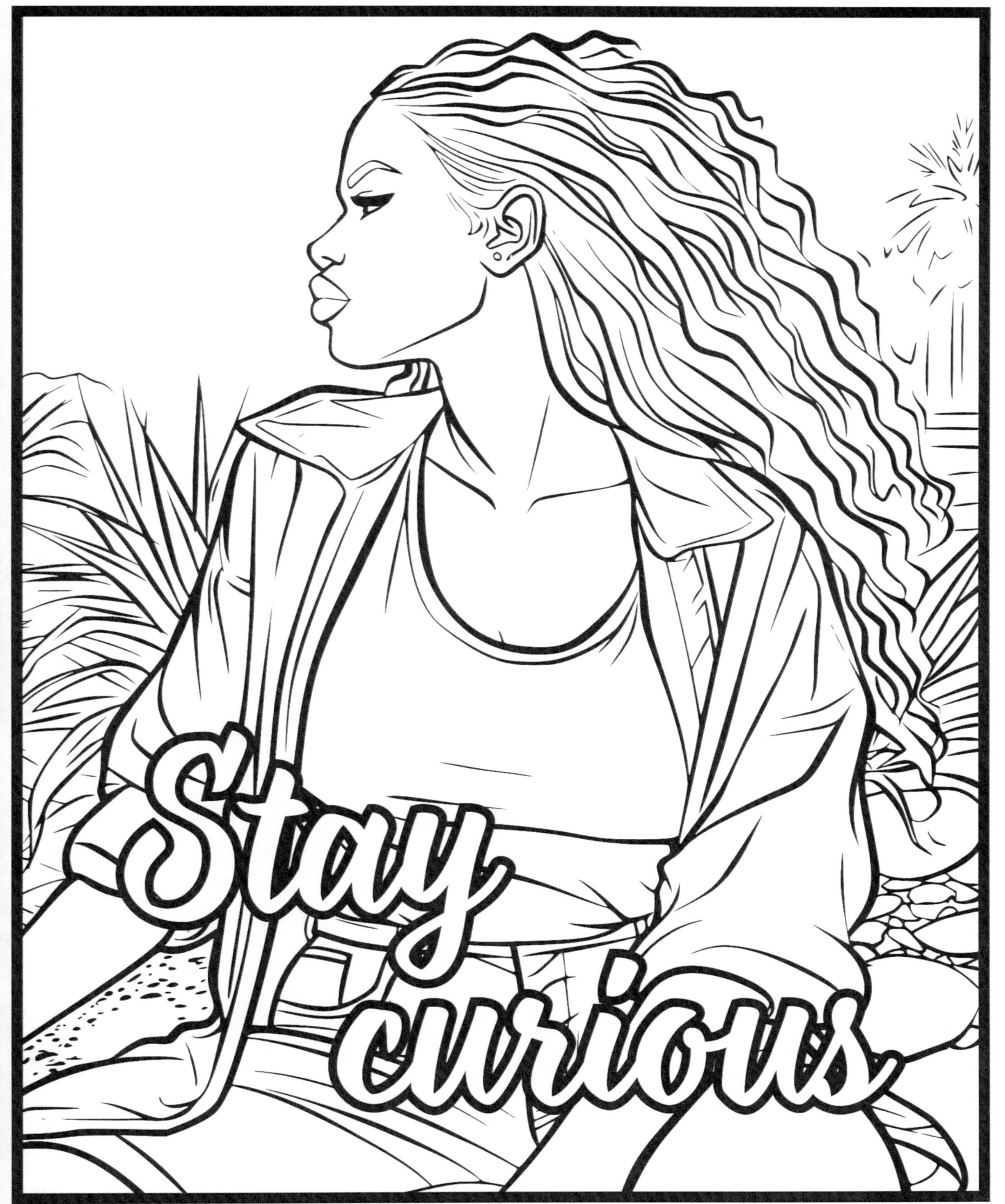

Stay
curious

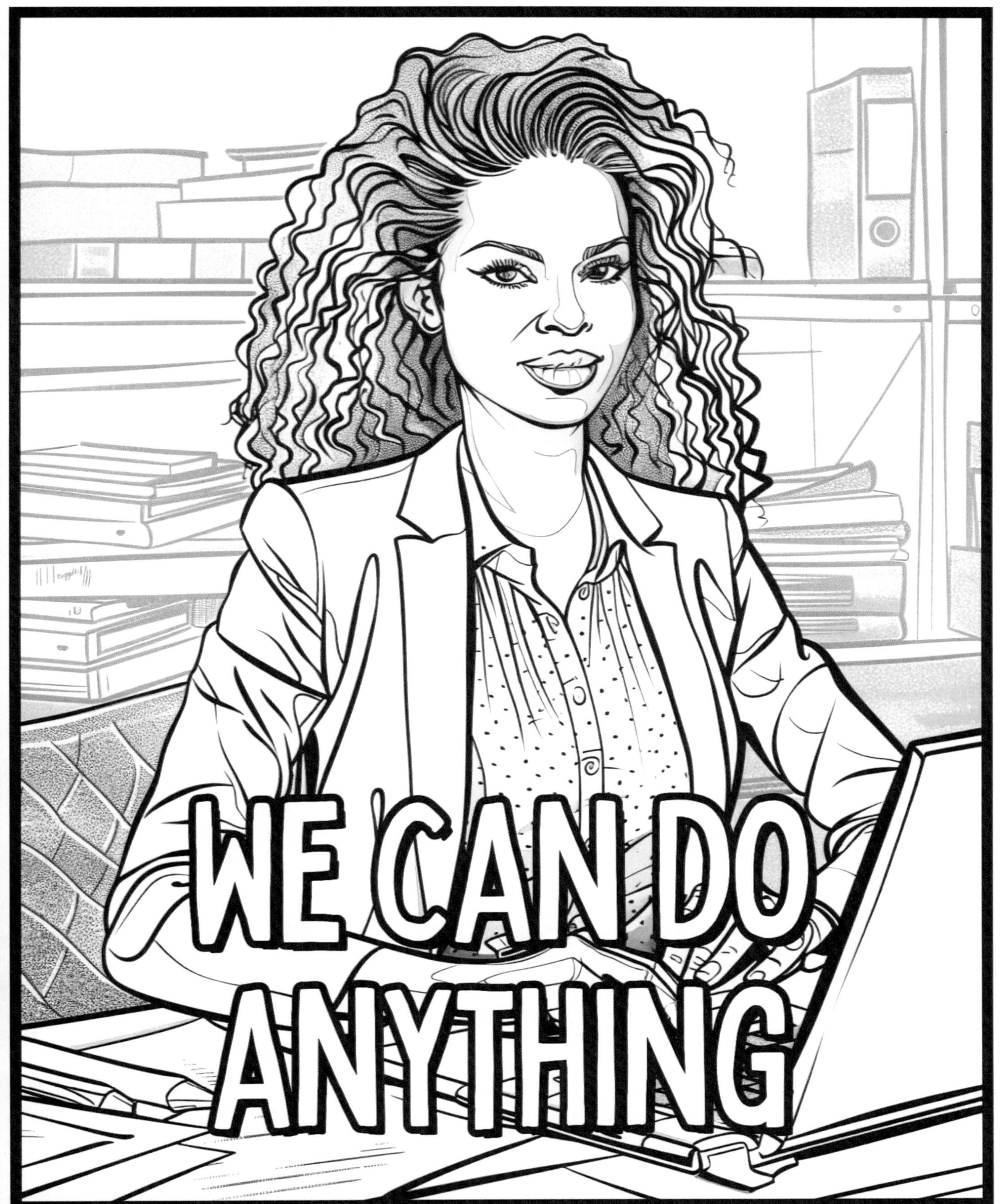

WE CAN DO ANYTHING

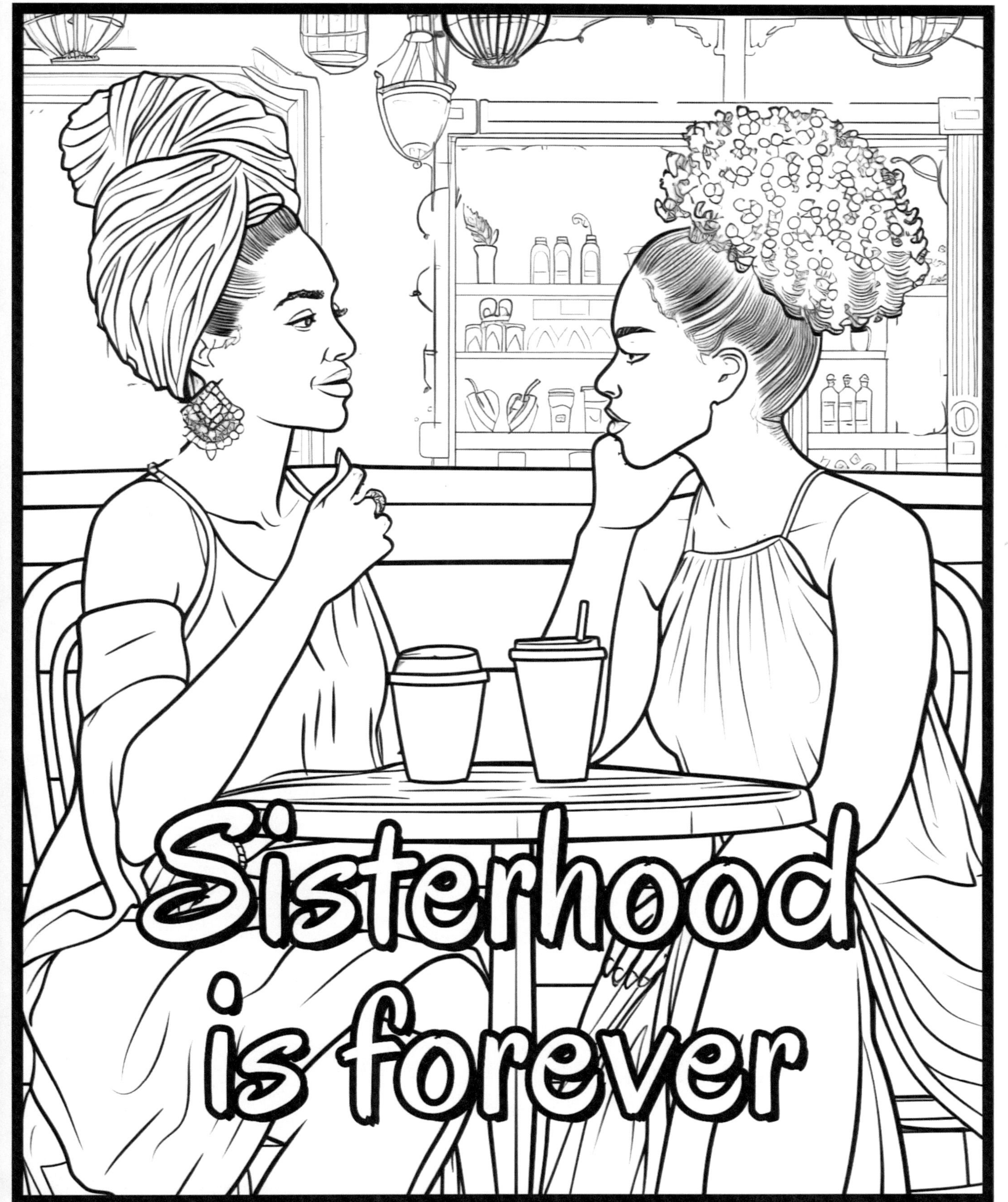

Sisterhood
is forever

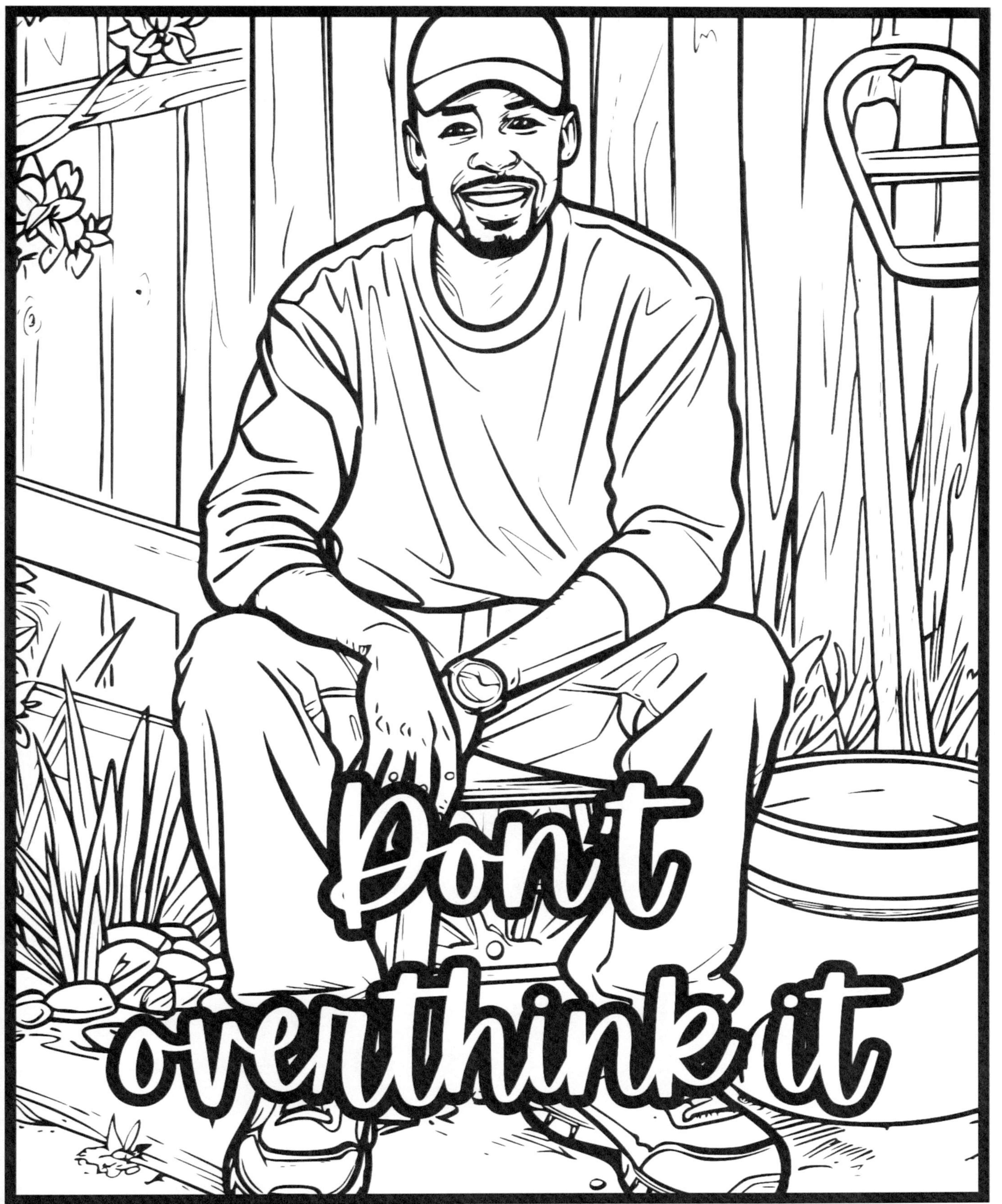

Don't
overthink it

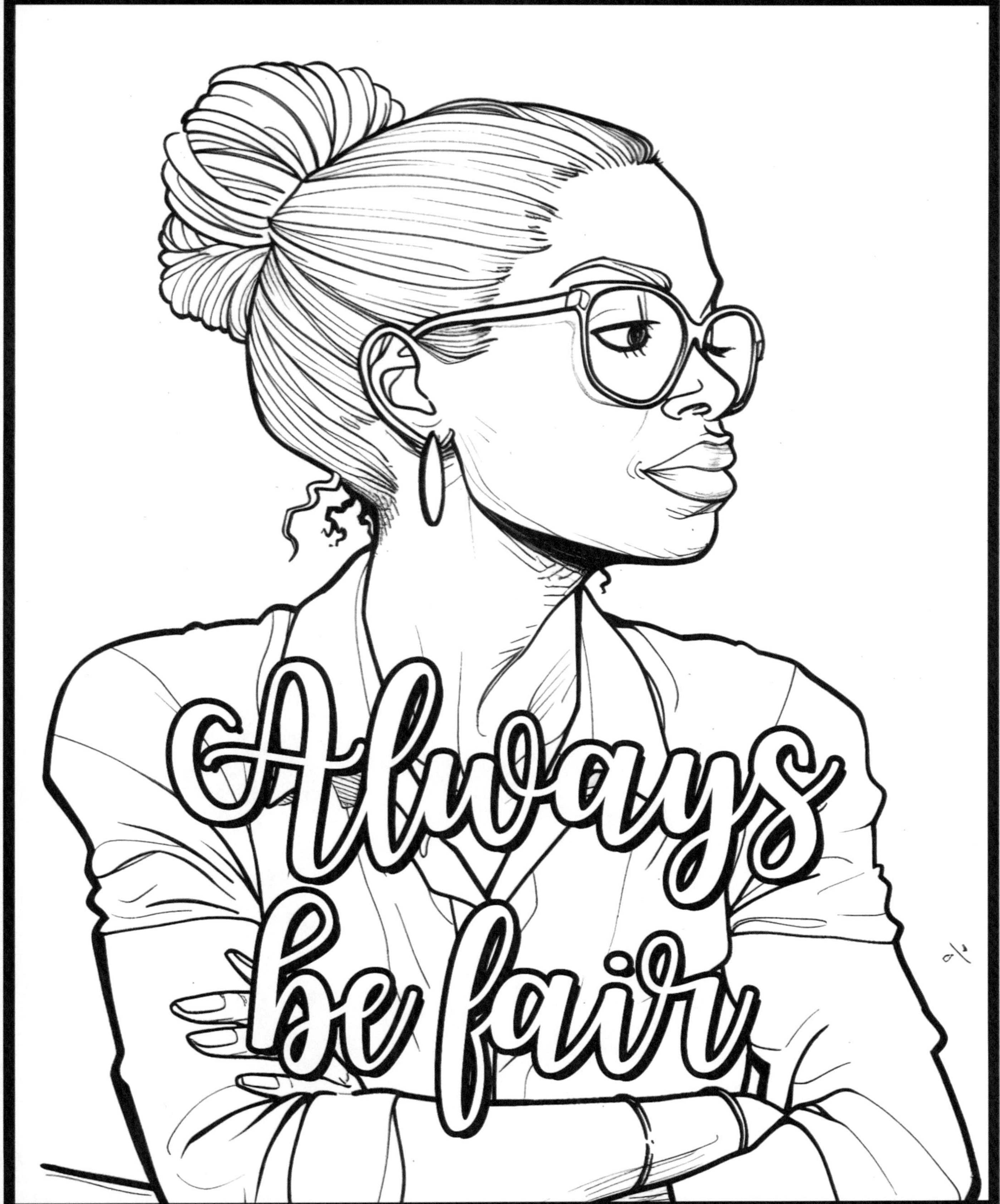

Always
be fair

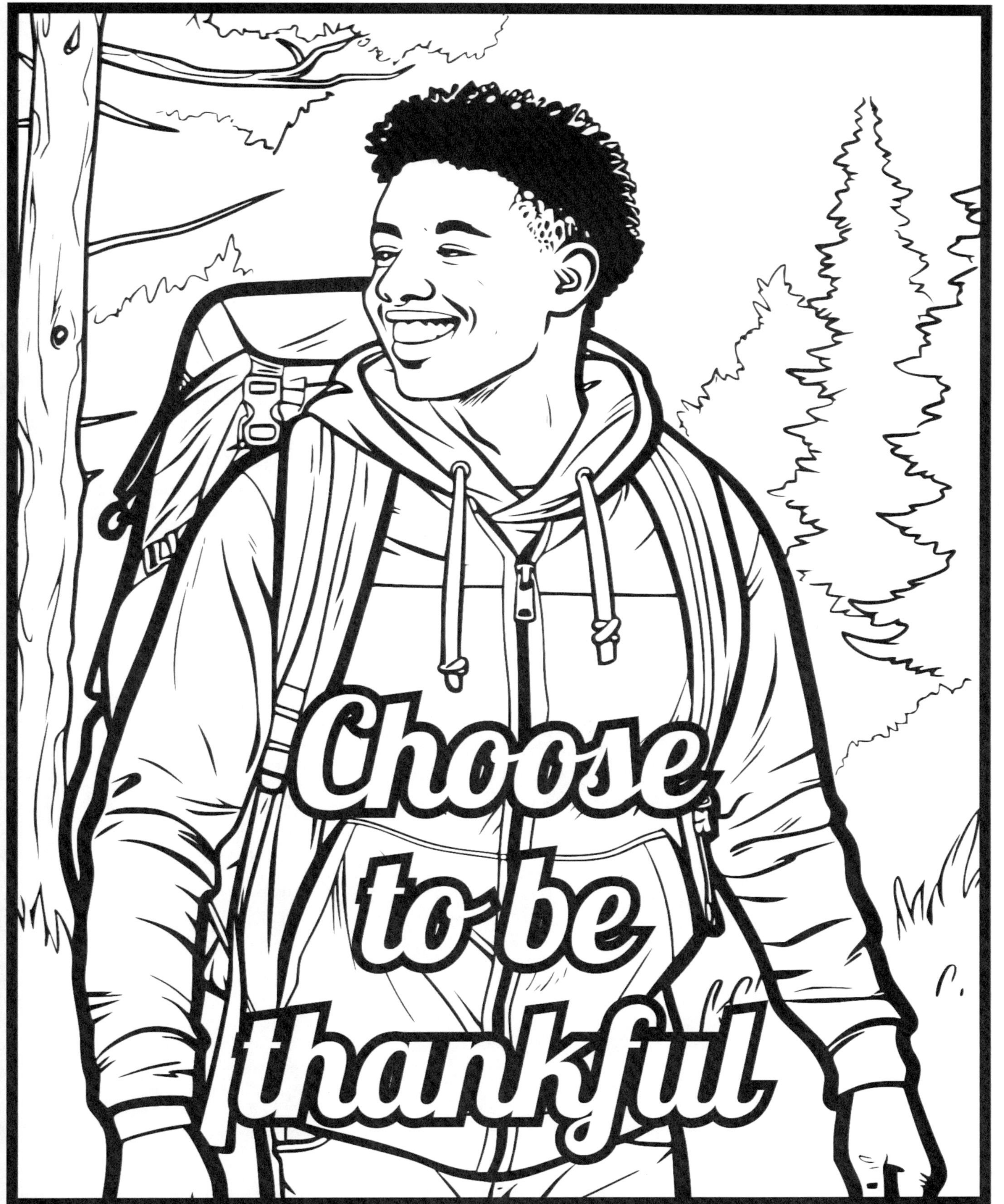

Choose
to be
thankful

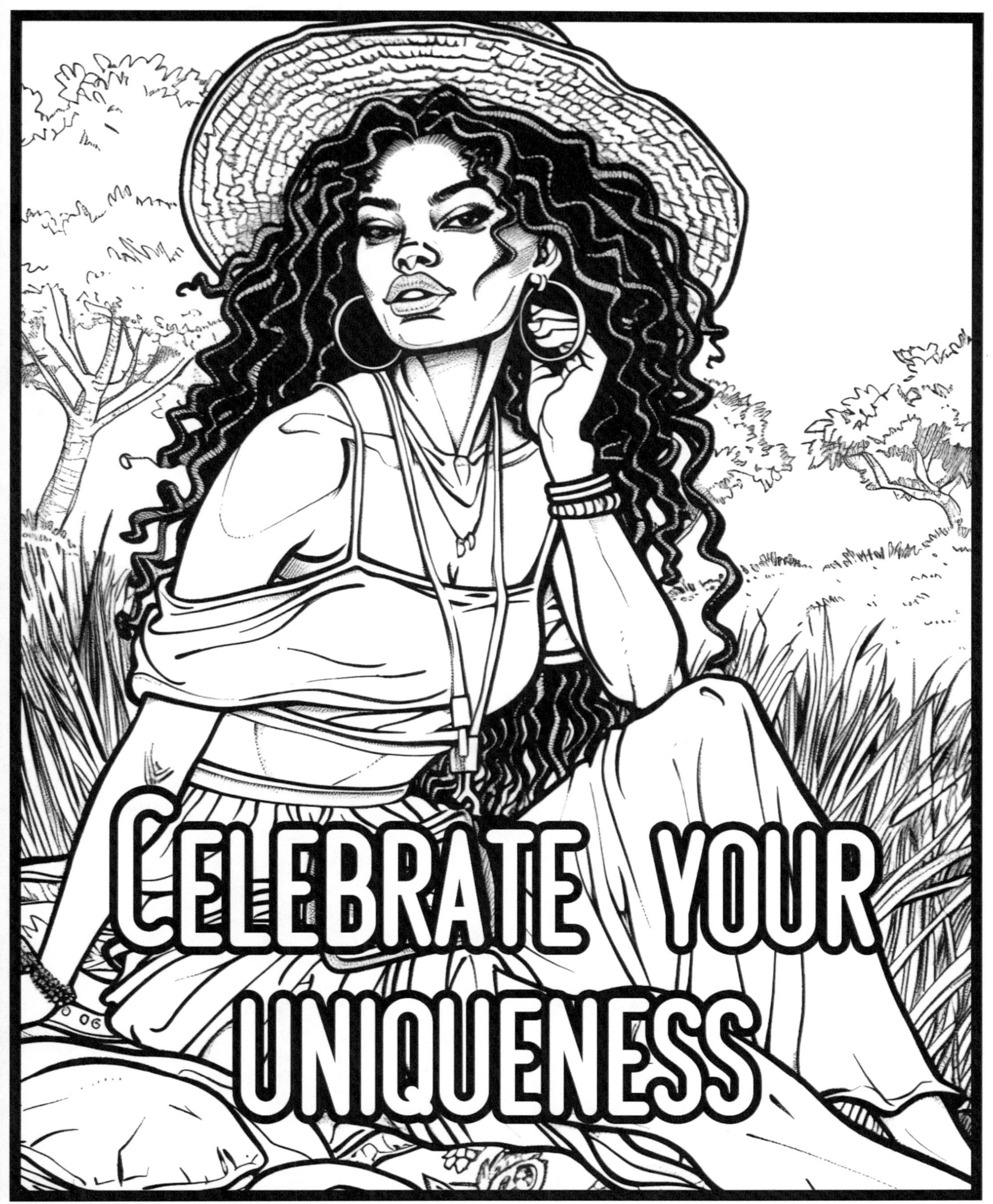

Celebrate your
uniqueness

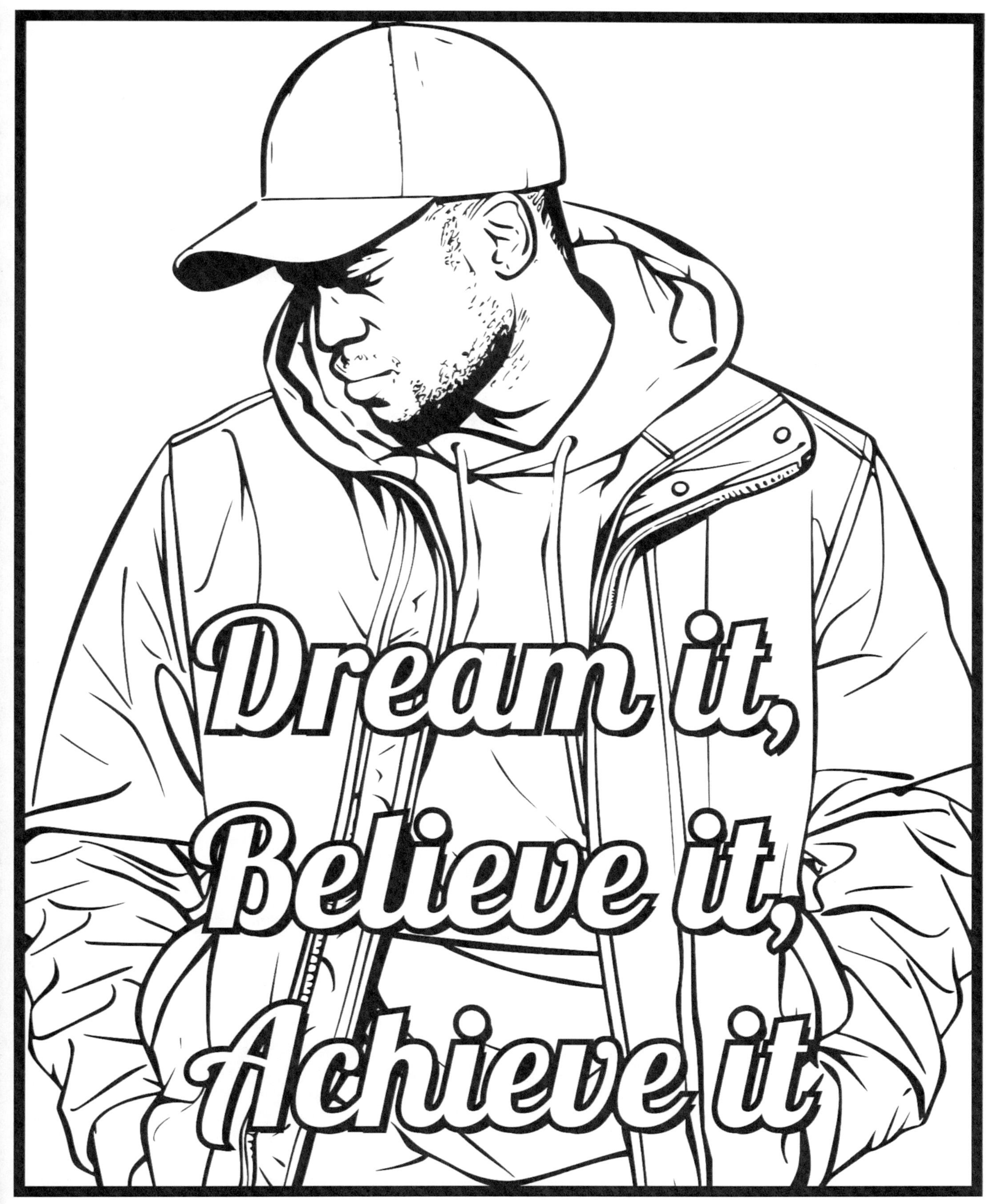
Dream it,
Believe it,
Achieve it

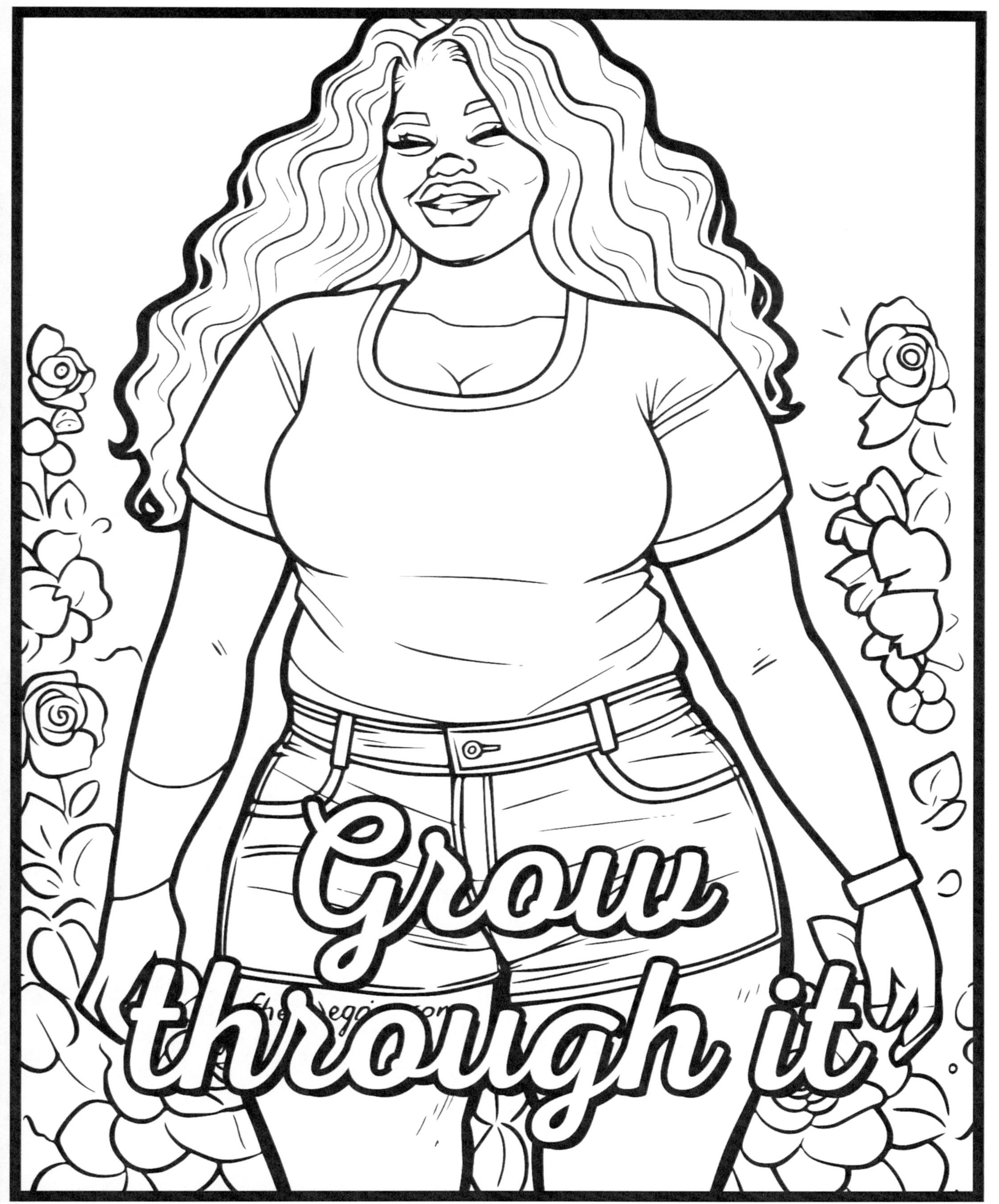

Grow
through it

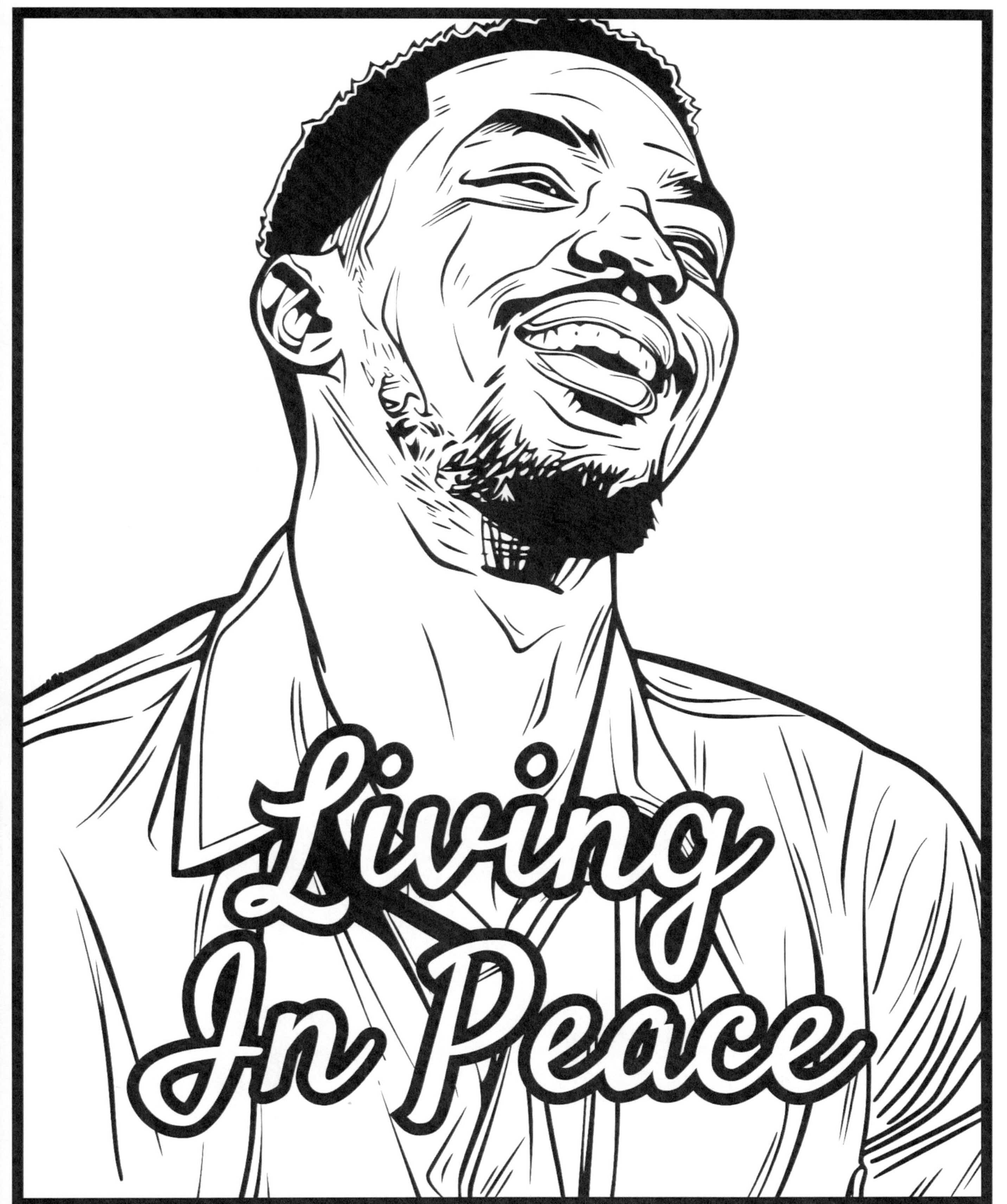

Living
In Peace

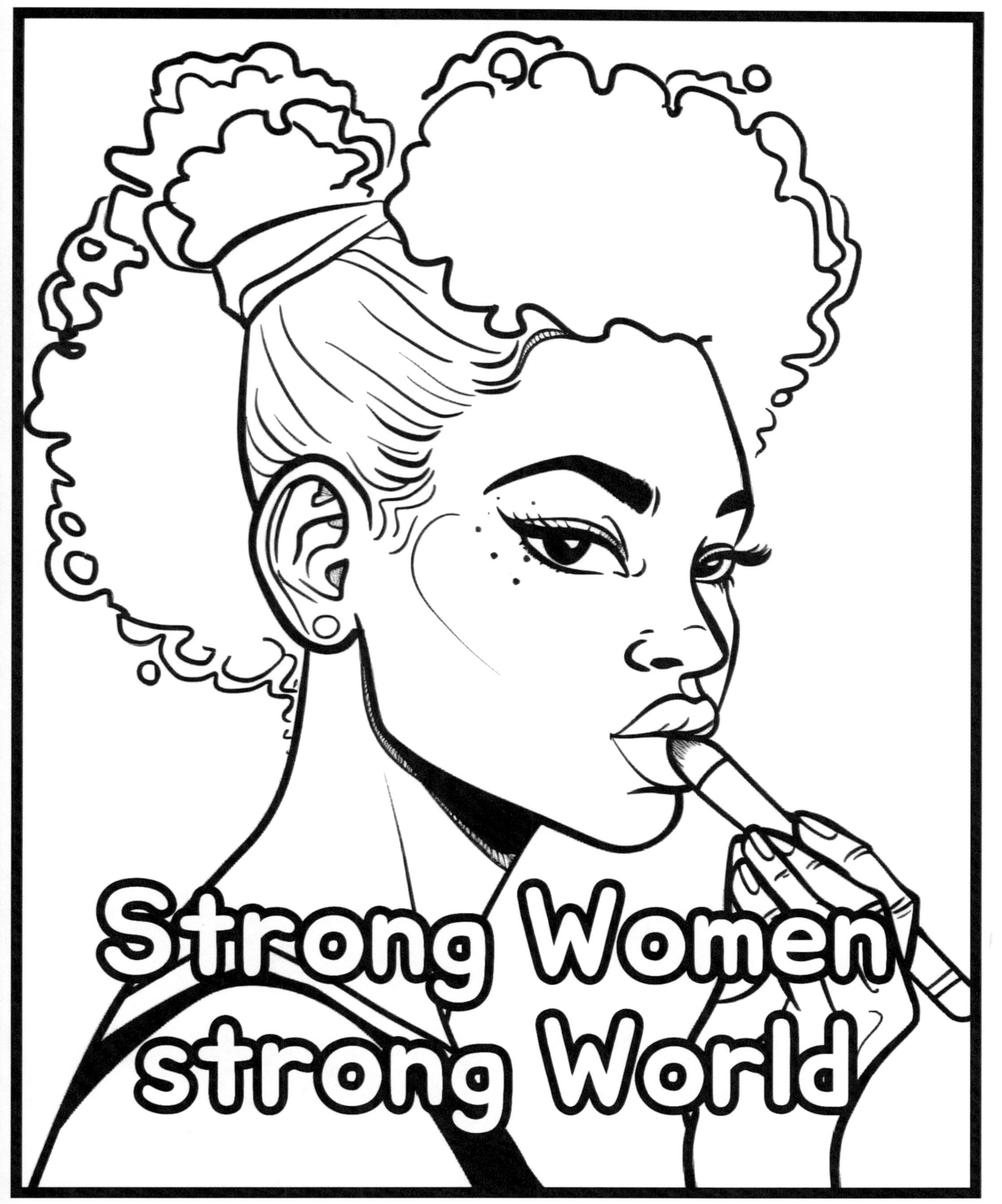

Strong Women
strong World

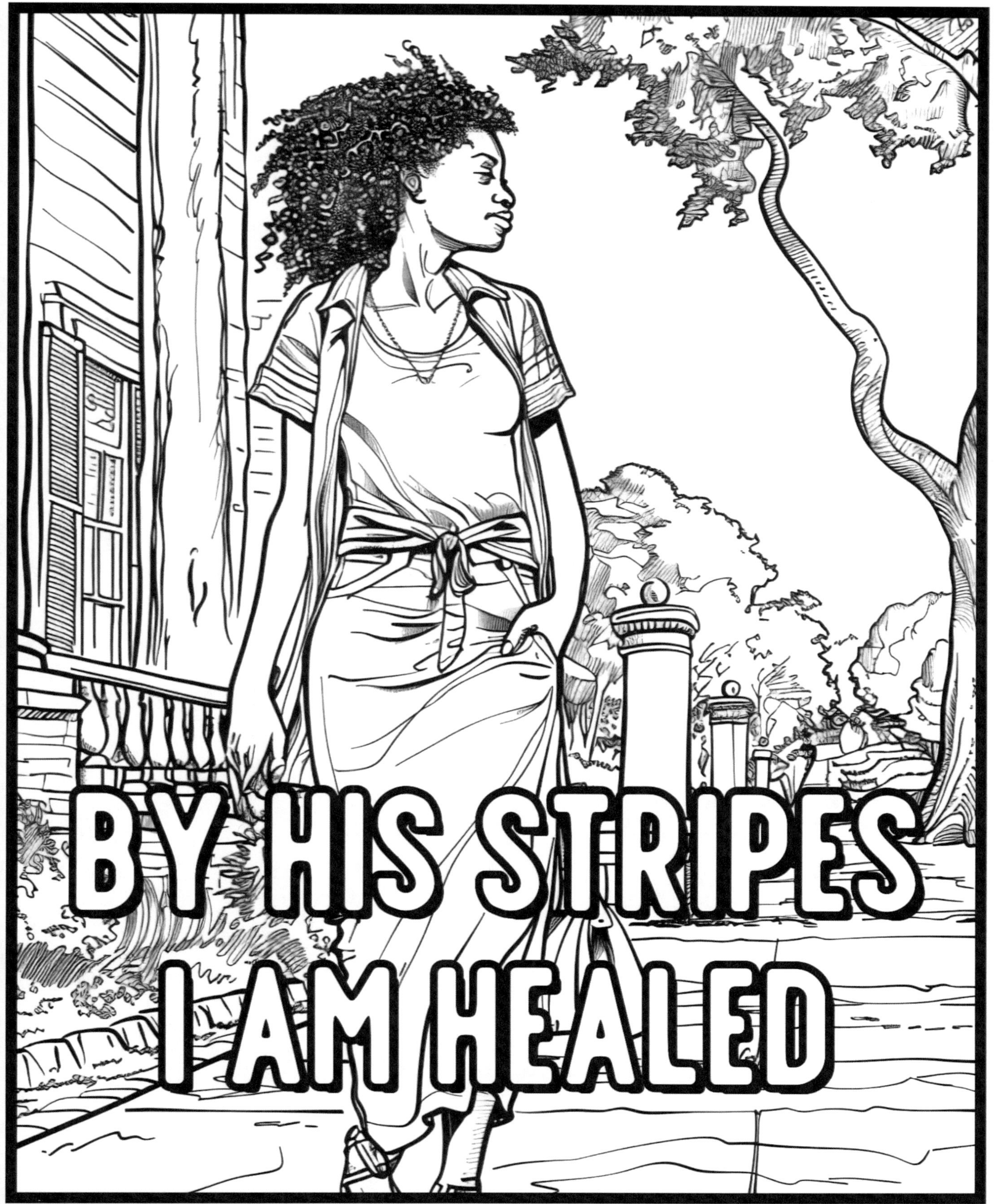

BY HIS STRIPES
I AM HEALED

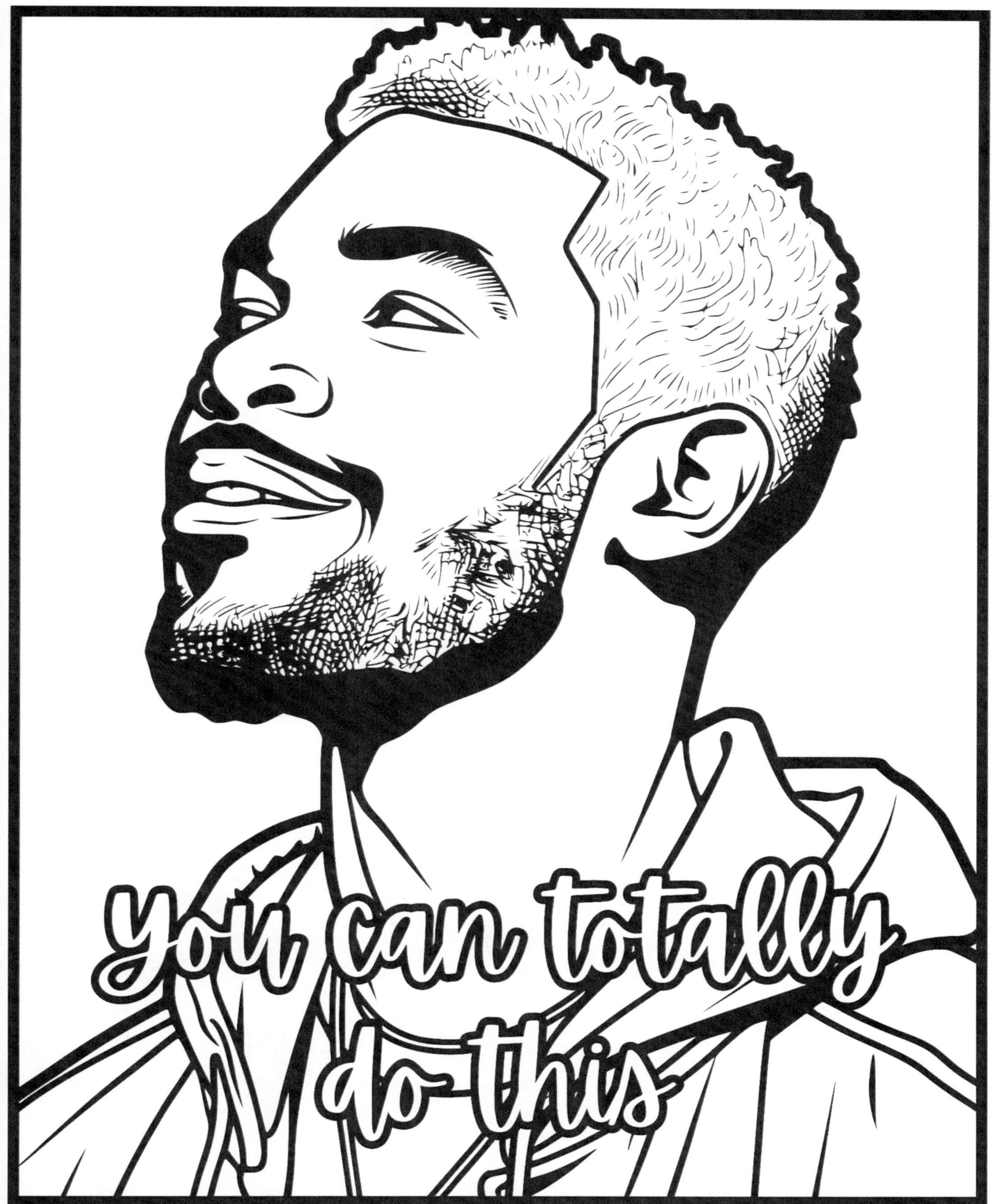

You can totally
do this

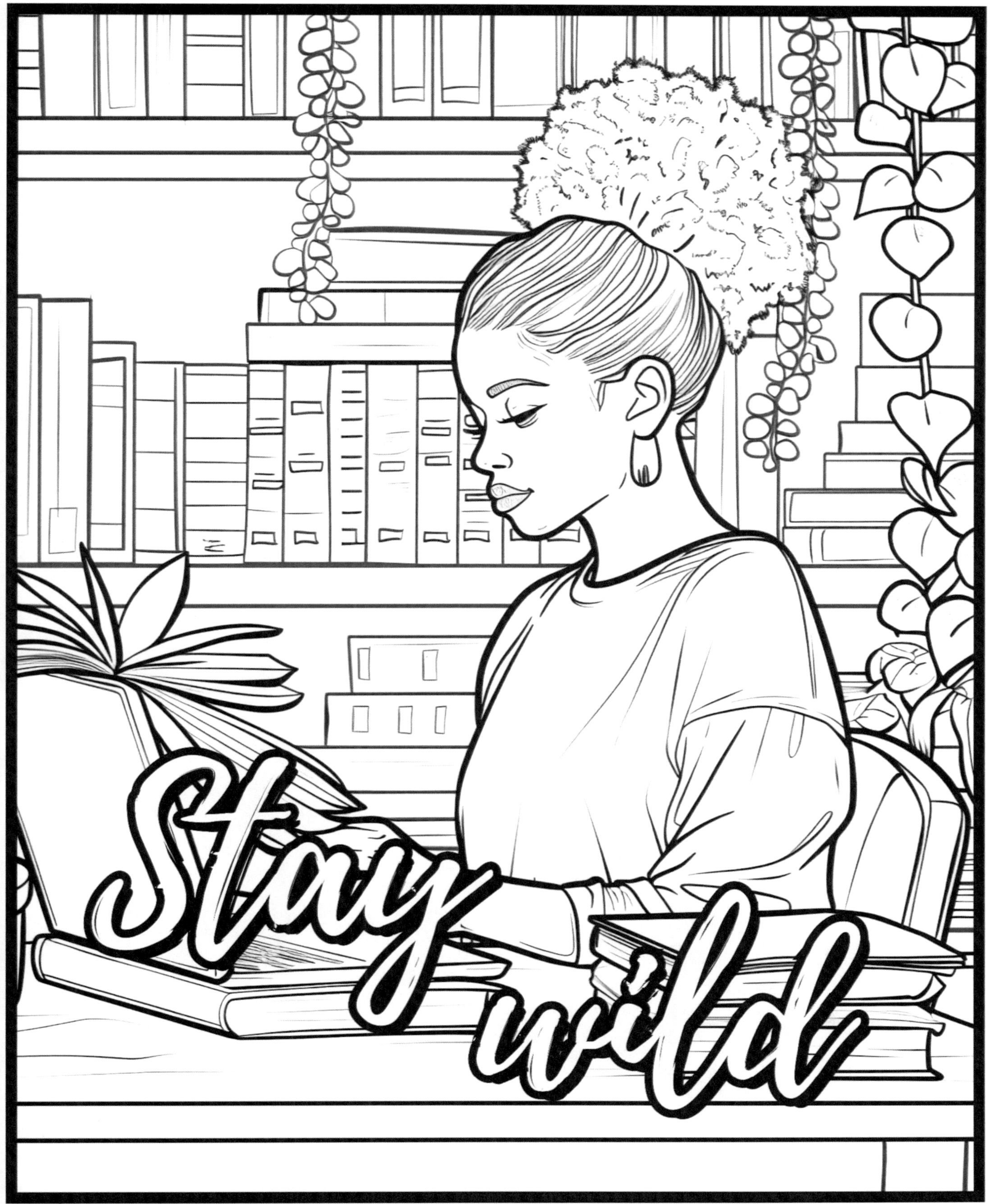

Stay
wild

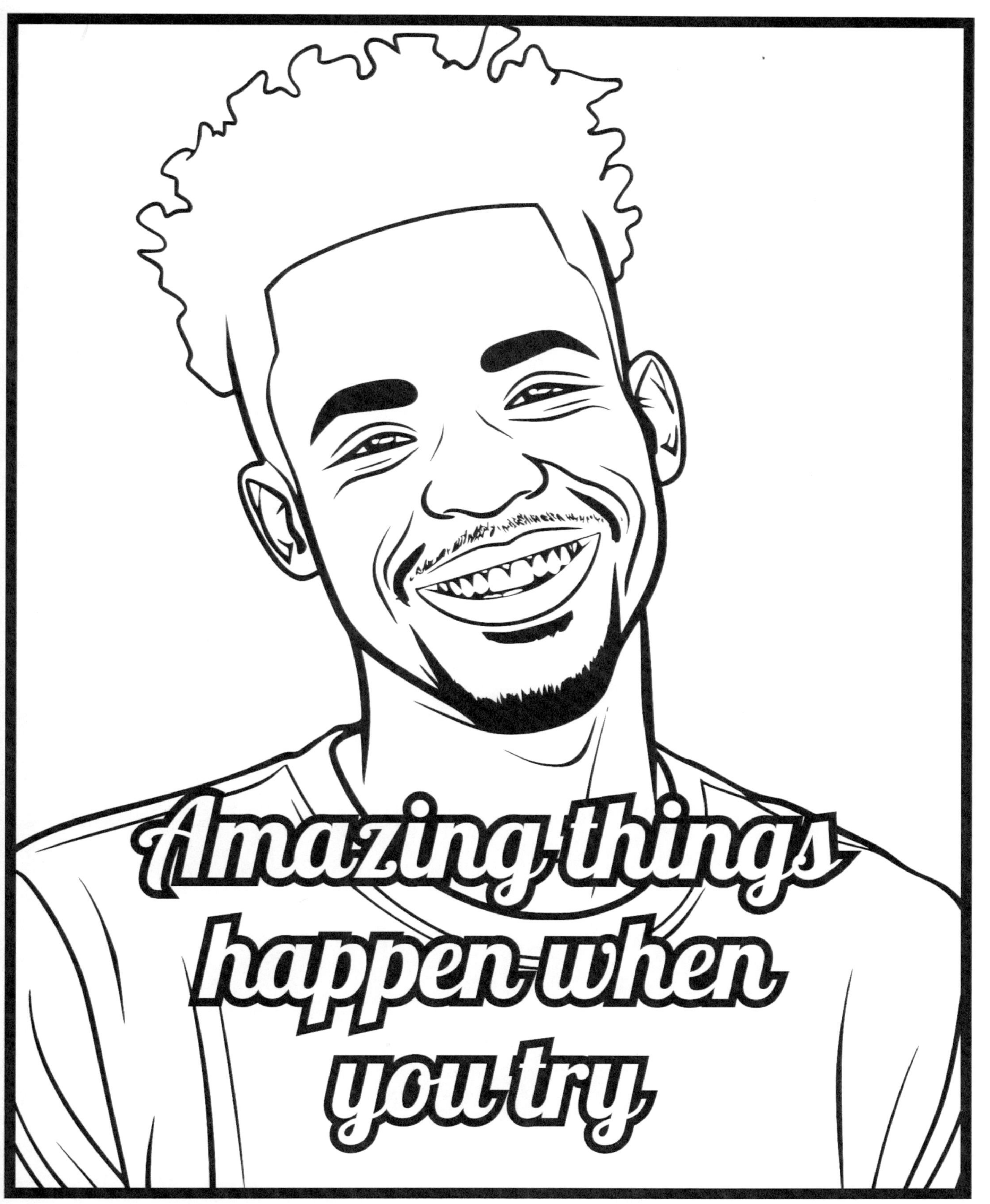
Amazing things happen when you try

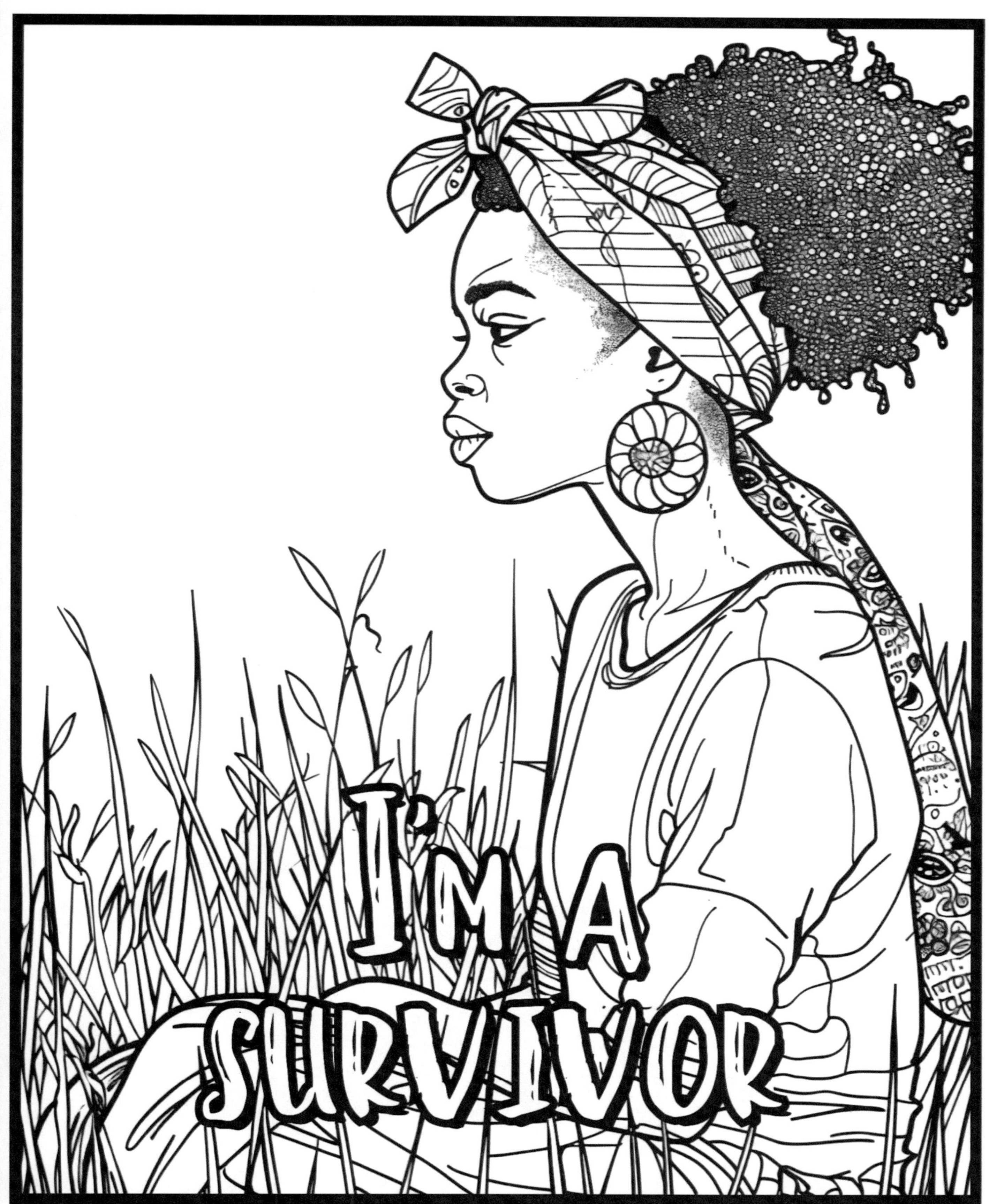

I'M A
SURVIVOR

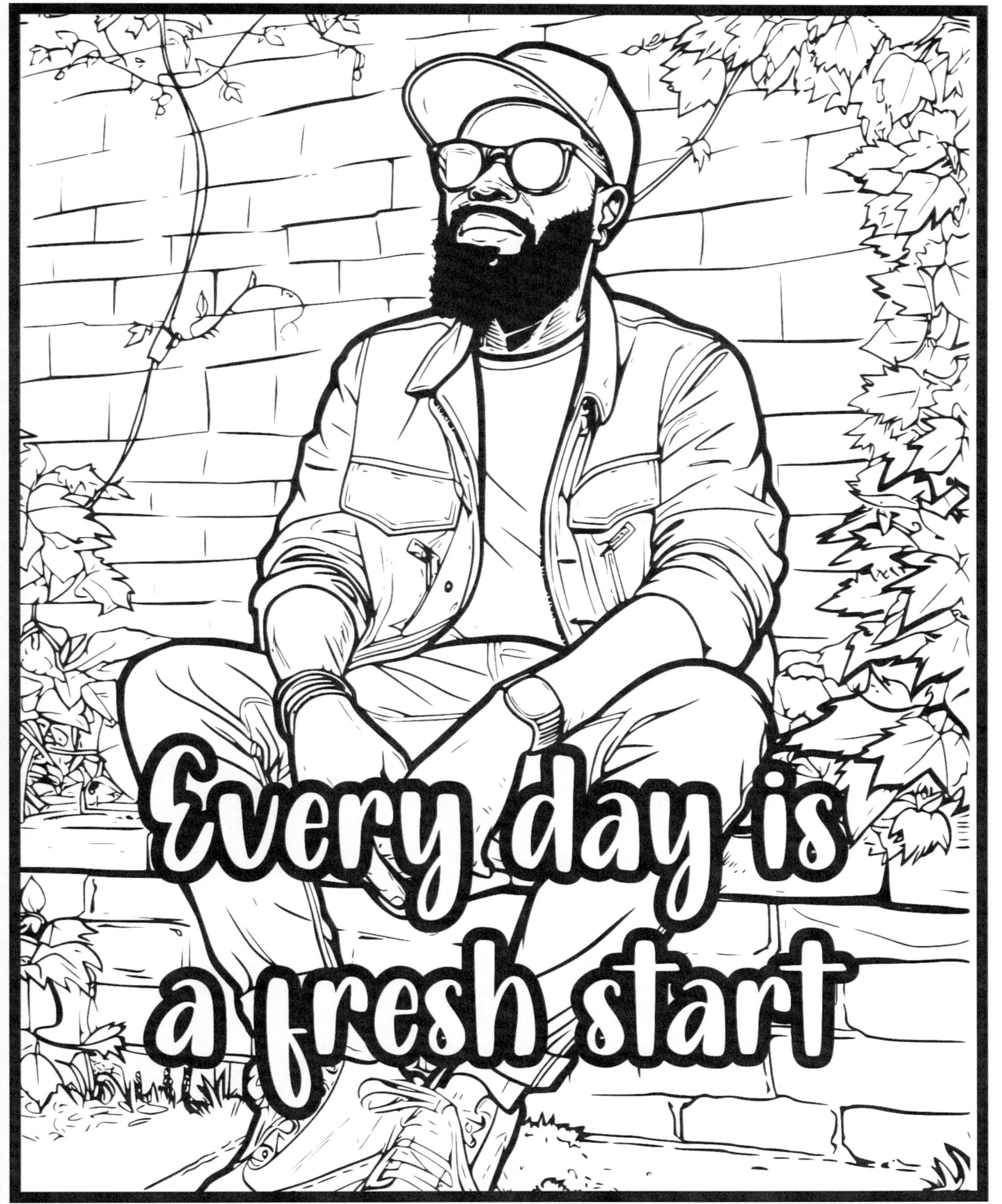

Every day is
a fresh start

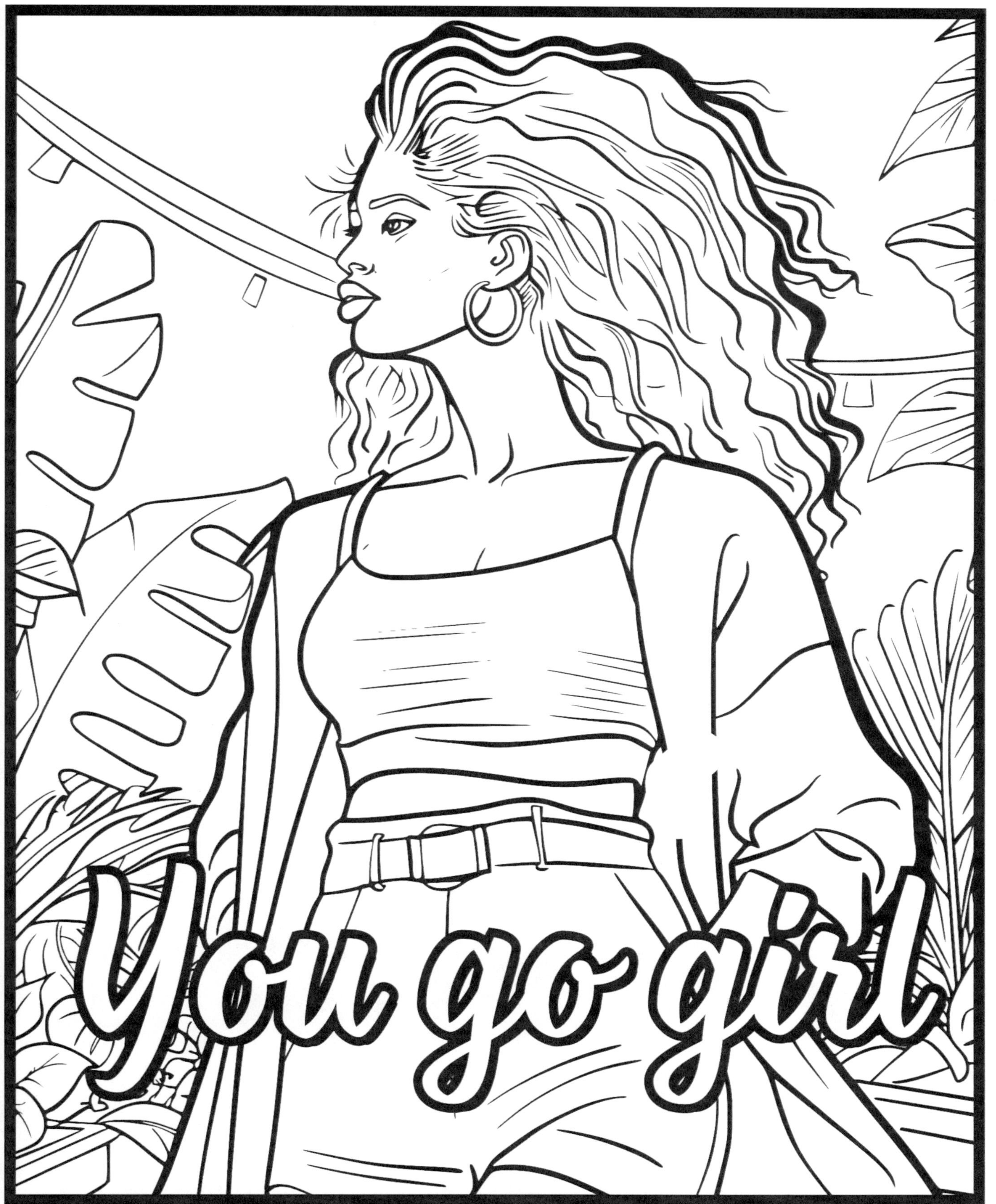

You go girl